S0-BQG-335

Etiquette

ETIQUETTE

Your Ticket to Good Times

by Helen Hoke

pictures by Carol Wilde

SOUTHOLD FREE LIBRARY,

CANCELLED

Franklin Watts, Inc.
575 Lexington Avenue
New York, N.Y. 10022

SBN 531-00686-7

Copyright © 1970 by Franklin Watts, Inc.
Library of Congress Catalog Card Number: 70-93223
Printed in the United States of America
1   2   3   4   5

Contents

27480

21480

Etiquette

What Is Etiquette?

Perhaps when you hear the word "etiquette" you think of bejeweled ladies in billowing gowns, curtsying at a royal court, or gentlemen dressed in velvet and lace, bowing before the queen. Those pictures actually come close to describing what etiquette used to mean hundreds of years ago.

"Étiquette" is a French word that means "ticket." In the days of the French kings, people had to have tickets to visit the palace. These tickets were given only to visitors who knew how to act properly, who understood the rules of social behavior, and who could speak nicely to other guests and to the royal hosts.

Today, etiquette still means good taste and manners. And, in a sense, it still means a "ticket." Knowing the rules of etiquette is your ticket to just about everywhere in the world. It means that you know just what to do and say without even thinking about it. Etiquette also means acting and speaking in such a way that people want to see you again, and enjoy inviting you to their homes.

The rules of etiquette are really quite simple if you remember that the reason for them is to make other people feel at ease. People are more likely to be friendly if you are friendly to them and thoughtful of their feelings.

You have already learned lots of rules right in your own home about being considerate of others. You know that you should not be selfish with such things as the family television set, the bathroom, or the record player. You know that you should sit up straight and behave well at the dinner table, and that you should be polite to your parents' guests and to your own.

But besides these simple rules for everyday living, there are rules for going to a party or giving one, for writing and accepting invitations, for introducing people, and for eating in other people's houses, where the service may be more formal than it usually is at your own dinner table. Do you know that manners for boys are sometimes different from manners for girls? Do you know how to answer the telephone correctly, or how to write a bread-and-butter letter?

(*10*)

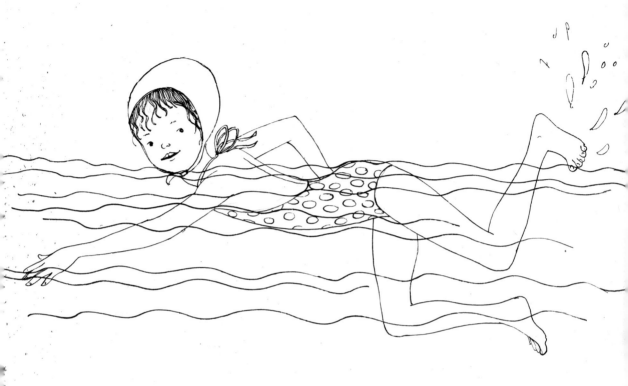

Remember when you first learned to swim or to ride a bicycle? At first you had to go through everything in slow motion until you got the knack of it. But now that you know how, you can swim or ride without even thinking about your hands and feet. They just act naturally.

(*11*)

And that is the way it is with etiquette. After just a little practice, you will do and say all the correct things without even thinking about them. You will have "instant manners," and you will also be someone that everyone likes to have around.

At the end of each section of this book, you will find a quizz to take to see how much you have learned. If your score is too low, read the chapter again and think about the *reasons* for the things you ought to do in any situation. When you have finished reading this book, take all the quizzes again, and see how high a mark you can get.

Hello!

Knowing how to introduce people properly is the first rule of etiquette. When you bring home a friend who has not met your parents or your brother or sister, you must introduce them. When you are with a friend and someone he has not met comes up to you — you also introduce them. When you are the host or hostess at a party, you introduce each guest who comes in to anyone he does not already know.

The first time that you read the rules for introductions you may be a little confused. But read them through again until you understand which person's name to say first.

You always say a distinguished person's name before that of a lesser-known person.
You always say a grown-up's name before a child's; a woman's name before a man's;

a girl's name before a boy's; and

an older person's name before that of a younger person
of the same sex.

For instance, your mother's name will always come first, whether you are introducing a boy or a girl, a man or a woman, *except* when you introduce her to such persons as a woman teacher, a clergyman, or a friend's mother.

When you introduce a friend to your mother, you say:

"Mother, this is my friend, George Parsons. Georgie, this is my mother."

When you introduce a friend of yours to another friend of about the same age, you say:

"Mary, this is John Bates. John, this is Mary Topping."

In a more informal way, you might say:

"Mary Topping, I'd like you to meet John Bates."

After the introduction, it is also a good idea to mention some interest that the two people may have in common — dogs, swimming, or perhaps stamp collecting — so that they will have something to talk about right away if they are left alone.

If you are introducing George Parsons to your younger brother, George's name is mentioned first because he is older. But if you introduce George to your sister, her name will be mentioned first.

(*15*)

"Jane, this is George Parsons. George, my sister Jane."

When two boys are being introduced, they shake hands. But when one boy is being introduced to a girl, it is considered good manners for him to wait until she offers her hand. If she does not, they both just smile and say "Hello!" As they grow older, "How do you do?" becomes a more accepted phrase.

If you do shake hands with someone, make sure that your handshake is firm, not too hard or soft. People don't like to have their hands crushed, but they don't like to feel that they are holding a wet fish either.

When you introduce George to your aunt, you should say her last name so that George will know what to call her. For instance:

"Aunt Amy, this is my friend, George Parsons. George, my aunt, Mrs. Martin."

You do not have to mention your mother's last name when you introduce her, unless she has remarried and her name now is different from yours.

These are the most usual kinds of introductions you will need to make. If the rules seem a bit confusing, make a game out of them with a group of friends. Pin a label on each one — "minister," "mother," "teacher," "girl cousin," or "playmate." Then each one in turn can introduce all the others.

You'll all make some mistakes at first, but if you start practicing now, introductions will soon become second-nature to you. Knowing how to introduce people properly will give you confidence so that you can enjoy parties and guests, and glide through social situations as smoothly as you glide along on your bike.

Know-Your-Introductions Quiz

As the first part of an introduction, do you say:

1. "Georgie, here's my mother."
2. "Ann, may I present my grandmother."
3. "Dad, this is my friend Ann Holly."

(*19*)

4. "Hey, everybody, just introduce yourselves."
5. "Mother, this is my teacher, Miss Andrews."
6. "Mr. Calvert, this is Senator Briggs."
7. "Dr. Olsen, this is my sister Jean."
8. "Father Kelly, this is my mother."

Now turn the page upside down and see what your score is. If you have

8 right: You know all the rules and never make a mistake.

5-7 right: Very good. But read and practice just a little bit more.

1-4 right: Not very good. Read the chapter over and over, and practice with your friends or at home.

None right: Perhaps you should ask your mother to go over this chapter with you and explain it until you understand.

ANSWERS
1. N
2. N
3. Y
4. N
5. N
6. N
7. Y
8. Y

Table Manners

> A child should always say what's true
>
> And speak when he is spoken to,
>
> And behave mannerly at table;
>
> At least as far as he is able.

This is a verse by Robert Louis Stevenson that you may have heard before.

Your mother has probably been telling you about table manners ever since you came down off your high chair and joined the others at the dinner table. So you already know some of the rules.

Here are some simple ones that you are familiar with:

Sit up straight; do not balance on the back legs of your chair.

Do not wave your knife and fork around or stick them up in the air or bang them on the plate or the table.

Do not hold your knife and fork upright in your fist, like a dagger ready to stab someone.

Eat slowly, with your mouth closed. Don't gulp or make noises. Sip your milk or water quietly, and never make gurgling sounds through a straw. (It's fun, but it isn't etiquette.)

Ask politely for something to be passed to you — salt, or another helping — do not reach across the table for it.

But you already know all *these* things, don't you?

When you are invited to your friend's house for dinner you may find that his family's arrangements are more formal than yours — especially if you are invited to a dinner party and there are several other guests. That is why you should know how a formal place setting looks, and exactly what to do with everything.

Here is the etiquette for dining out — a great and a fun occasion!

Place settings vary a little according to what food is going to be served. For instance, if the first course is soup, the soup plate probably will already be on the table when you go into the dining room. But perhaps the dinner will begin

(22)

with a shrimp or fruit cocktail or an artichoke. Then other kinds of dishes will be needed.

But certain things will always be the same:

The fork, or forks, will always be at the left of the dinner plate. At the right, from the inside out, will be the knives and then the spoons.

There is no need to be confused about finding a lot of silverware at your place, for this rule is the simplest one of all: *always use the one at the outside first.* (If your first course is soup, you will find the soup spoon at your far right. If it is a shrimp cocktail, you will find a tiny fork at your far left.)

As you can see from the diagram, the butter plate and butter knife are placed above the forks, and the glass is above the knives. Napkins are usually placed at your left, but some hostesses fold them on top of the dinner plate.

Younger guests wait for adults to be seated first. As soon as you sit down, unfold your napkin halfway and put it in your lap. Then wait for your hostess to begin eating. It is very impolite for a guest to begin first, and besides, if you are in any doubt about which fork or spoon to use, you can watch her and do the same.

When you are not eating — when you pause to take a drink of water or to talk to someone — your knife and fork should be placed like this:

and when you have finished a course, place your knife and fork like this —

— so that your hostess can tell that you have finished eating.

Your bread and butter are, of course, on your bread and butter plate, and the butter knife must stay there, too. *Break* off just a portion of bread at a time, and butter it. Never take up a full slice to eat.

When someone passes a dish to you, take the portion nearest you and then pass it on to the next person. If a maid is serving, she will stand at your left so that you can help yourself with your right hand.

Do not reach for the pickles, the gravy, or the salt if they are not in front of you. Instead, ask the person nearest the dish you want to pass it to you, and be sure to say *please*.

(25)

When you leave the table, place your napkin (without folding it again) to the left of your place. Never leave the table before the others do. But if you must, say "May I be excused, please?" and slip away quietly.

When you are dining out, eat a little of everything that is passed to you. You may think that you do not like strange things such as artichokes or turtle soup or oysters or curry — but you may have a pleasant surprise. Millions of people have learned to love unusual food after taking "two bites for politeness." Besides, refusing your hostess's food is *not etiquette*! But if there is something you particularly like, do tell her.

Table manners are really easy because they make sense.

Know-Your-Table-Manners Quiz

Do you:

1. Sit down as soon as you have been told which is your chair?

2. Put your napkin on your lap as soon as you sit down?

3. Choose your fork by size, according to the kind of food on your plate?

4. Put your fork beside your plate when you've finished eating?

5. Take the largest portion of food on the platter handed to you?

6. Ask for something you want to be passed to you?

7. Try things that you don't think you like?

8. Tell your hostess that you like the food, if you do?

Now turn the page upside down and see what your score is. If you have

8 right: You will be a welcome guest any time!

5-7 right: You are making a few mistakes. Better polish up your table manners!

1-4 right: Oh, dear, your hosts probably won't invite you back until you learn the rules and practice them some more.

None right: Read the chapter very very carefully again, and ask your mother to explain the parts you don't understand. Practice at your dinner table at home.

(29)

ANSWERS
1. N
2. Y
3. N
4. N
5. N
6. Y
7. Y
8. Y

A Weekend Away from Home

You have been invited to spend a weekend at your friend's house. It will be your first weekend away from home without a member of your family. Of course, you think about all the fun you'll have — swimming or playing baseball or going on a picnic or meeting his other friends. You might have so much fun that you will want to be invited back. But you will be invited back by your friend's parents only if you show that you know the etiquette of being a house guest.

First of all, pack your suitcase with everything you will need. Otherwise you will arrive and find that you have to borrow a comb, a pair of sneakers, or a clean pair of socks. You must bring your own toilet articles, and all the clean clothes that you will need for the activities planned. So, Rule

1 is *Come prepared.* But don't bring all your toys and possessions and look as if you are prepared to spend three months.

When you arrive, say hello to your friend's parents and thank them for letting you come. (Be friendly to his brothers and sisters, aunts and uncles, cats and dogs, and any other members of the household, too. Make them all glad that you're there.)

You will be shown where you are to sleep and where the bathroom is. Unpack your clothes and put them away in the space that has been saved for you. Don't drop them on the floor and start the weekend with a clutter.

You may be shown other parts of the house that you can use, such as a playroom or family room, but remember that all other rooms are *off limits.* Never go into anyone else's bedroom, nor even into the kitchen unless you are invited. This is not your own house to roam about in as you please. And never go into a room with a closed door without knocking first.

The next rule is to follow the schedule of the house and do whatever has been planned for you. *Never* say, "Let's have lunch," or, "Let's go to the beach now." It is up to your hosts to tell you what time meals are and what activities are planned, and it's up to you to join in cheerfully.

If they want to play games that you don't know, say that

you would love to learn. If the family wants to listen to records that you don't like, listen politely to them, and don't *say* that you don't like them.

Before each meal, be sure to excuse yourself to go and wash your hands and face and comb your hair. Your friend's mother may not *ask* you to, but she will certainly *want* you to. It is etiquette to come to the table looking clean and neat.

It really is *fun* to go visiting. Review all the table-manner rules in the last chapter so that you will behave like a person thoroughly accustomed to going visiting! Join in the conversation. Don't do *all* the talking, but on the other hand, don't be so busy eating or playing that you haven't time to say anything at all. (They invited you because they wanted your company.)

Your hostess may tell you that you are free to raid the refrigerator, but if you do, just take small snacks or a glass of milk or a soft drink. Don't cut into the roast that might be intended for tomorrow's dinner.

Your own parents may allow you to stay up until quite late on weekend nights, but your friend's parents may expect you to go to your room an hour or so earlier because that is the rule in *their* house. Don't look cross or say that you don't want to go. Get up quickly, say goodnight, and trot off to bed — making sure that you wash thoroughly

(*33*)

or take a bath or shower. (People like to think that *clean* guests come to stay with them.)

If you are called the next morning, hurry on down to breakfast with a cheerful "good morning!" to everyone, even though you would rather go on sleeping. After all, they might have an exciting picnic planned, and everyone has to be ready to make an early start. If you are staying more than one night, make your bed, or smooth it out as well as you can, before leaving your room. Be sure that you haven't dropped your pajamas on the floor or left a damp towel wadded up in the corner.

If you have been playing, joining in all the activities planned for you, and being cheerful and saying "please" and "thank you," the way you know you should, then you are almost certain to be invited back again. Only a couple of simple rules are left:

When the visit is over, tell your friend's mother what a nice time you had, and thank her for letting you come. (And thank your friend, of course.) Then, when you get home, write your hostess a little note and thank her all over again. Maybe that sounds unnecessary, but it really ought to be done. See the pages in this book on writing letters for an easy way to write your bread-and-butter letter.

And be sure that you pack up all your belongings when

you leave so that your friend's mother doesn't have to wrap them up and mail them along after you.

Just turn this whole chapter topsy-turvy, and always remember that your friend may be making *his* first visit away from home. He may not know all the right things to do. Try to make him feel at ease, and a part of your family. If he makes any mistakes, don't mention them. Good manners for a host is making your guest feel welcome — never uncomfortable.

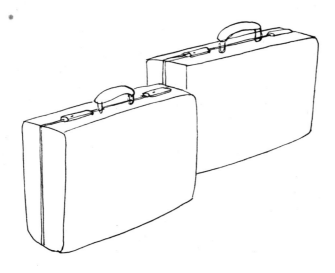

Know-How-to-Go-on-a-Weekend-Away-from-Home Quiz

Do you:

1. Say hello to everyone when you arrive?
2. Tell them exactly what you want to do and when?
3. Acquaint yourself with the house by making a tour of all the rooms?
4. Play games that are suggested, and ask to be taught the rules if you don't know them?
5. Tell them what kind of food you like so they will know what to have for dinner?

6. Wait for your hostess to unpack your bag for you?

7. Clean yourself up before you come to the table?

8. Go to bed when you're told?

Now turn the page upside down and find out what your score is. If you have:

8 right: You'll certainly be invited back, and you'll have a very good time, besides.

5-7 right: You might have done a few things wrong. Read the chapter again to see why.

1-4 right: You will probably not be invited back very soon. They'll wait until you've polished your visiting etiquette.

None right: Pretend that you're a guest in your *own* home, and ask your mother to tell you when you do things wrong. That's the way to learn.

ANSWERS
1. Y
2. N
3. N
4. Y
5. N
6. N
7. Y
8. Y

Party Time

Giving a party

Giving a party can be great fun, whether it is a birthday celebration, Halloween, Christmas, Valentine Day, or any other time. But a party will be *more* fun if you plan it carefully.

Select the date and the time, talking over your plans with your mother to make sure that the date does not interfere with other family plans.

Start making lists:

A list of games to play, a list of prizes to buy, a list of party favors, such as paper hats and noisemakers, and a list of refreshments — ice cream and cake, and — if it's a barbecue — hot dogs and hamburgers and all the things that go on them.

(*39*)

The most important list of all is the guest list. How
many? Boys *and* girls? Your classmates, neighbors, your
Scout troop? Don't ask more guests than you have room
for. Be sure to include new friends — and especially people
who have invited you to *their* parties. (This is called "re-
turning hospitality.")

Whether you invite your guests by mail, by phone, or in person, be sure to check off their names on your list when they accept so that your mother will know how many are coming. (You wouldn't want to run out of ice cream.)

When your party begins, greet your guests at the front door and show them where to put their coats. If it is a birthday party, each guest will probably bring a gift. Thank him when he gives it to you, and thank him again when you open it — whether you really like it or not.

You may have to introduce a new friend who doesn't know many people. You already know the rules for this. Remember — your new friend should first be introduced to your mother.

On party occasions you are allowed to make group introductions. If several of your guests have already arrived and the new girl in your class doesn't know any of them, you can say:

"This is Jane Pringle. Jane, this is Bob Brown, Jenny Cohen, Marjorie Kelly, and Jimmy Prentice," pointing them out as they stand around in a circle. All of them should smile and say hello and make a special effort to be nice to the stranger.

It's *your* party — you are the host or hostess — and it is up to you to see to it that everyone has a good time. Keep an eye out for anyone who looks left out, talk to him yourself, and manage to bring him into the game that is being played.

As host or hostess, you must play all the games. If you should win, it's not good manners to keep the prize. Give it to the boy or girl who has the next best score.

Going to a party

You already know about giving a party. Just as there are things that the party giver must do, so there are things that the party*goer* must do — so that it can be a wonderful party that people will talk about for weeks.

When you receive an invitation, let your host or hostess know as soon as possible whether you can come. If it is a birthday party, choose a gift that you know your friend will like and take it with you, wrapped in party paper, with a gift card, if possible.

A good guest joins in all the games. Even if there is a game you don't like, you will usually have more fun joining in than sitting and watching. Be especially nice to any strangers at the party. They may feel shy — and they might turn out to be your best friends in a little while.

The end of the party is the time for good-bye and thank you. When you notice that the other boys and girls are be-

(42)

ginning to leave, it is time for you to find your coat and leave, too. If for some reason it is necessary for you to leave the party early, explain why to your hostess.

Be sure to thank your friend *and* his mother, and to tell them what a nice time you had.

"Thanks, I had a wonderful time!"

Know-Your-Party Time Quiz

Do you:

1.   Ask your best friends and leave out the people who have invited you to their parties?

2.   Keep a list and check off who can come so you'll know how many there will be?

3.   Wait until after the party to open your presents?

4.   Leave the front door open and wait for your guests in the living room?

5.   Let your guests do what they like once they've been introduced?

6. If you win a prize, offer it to the runner-up?

7. If you're a guest, play all the games, whether you like them or not?

8. As a guest, always thank your hostess as well as your friend when you leave?

Now turn the page upside down and see what your score is. If you have:

8 right: You are a good partygoer and party giver and people will always like being with you.

5-7 right: Read the chapter again and find out why you made some mistakes.

1-4 right: You may not be invited back. Study all the ways of being a good guest.

None right: Read the chapter over, and practice "having a party" with just your brothers and sisters, or two close friends. This way you'll learn the rules.

ANSWERS

1. N
2. Y
3. N
4. N
5. N
6. Y
7. Y
8. Y

Writing Letters

Lots of people use the telephone for extending invitations and for accepting them. But knowing your etiquette means knowing how to write invitations and other kinds of letters. Here are a few examples:

An invitation to a party

Dear Tim,

   Can you come to my Fourth of July party at noon on the 4th? We're going to have a swim and a barbecue, so bring your bathing suit.

Sincerely,
Susan

R.S.V.P.

Those four letters at the bottom stand for a French phrase that means "reply if you please." It is used all over the world, whether people know French or not, and it means that you must let Susan know, as soon as possible, whether or not you can come. This is the note you might send:

Dear Susan,
 I'd love to come to your Fourth of July party. I'll be there at noon, with my bathing suit! Thank you for inviting me.

Sincerely,
Tim

Weekend invitations and acceptances contain a little more information:

Dear Tim,
 Can you come and spend the weekend from Friday the 4th to Sunday the 6th? We'll look for you in the afternoon. We're going to swim and fish and have a picnic on the beach Saturday night! I hope you can come.

Sincerely,
Pete

When you receive this note you know exactly what kind of clothes to bring, and just when you're expected to arrive and leave. And so you write something like this:

Dear Pete,

Thanks for your invitation. The fishing and the picnic sound great! Mom will put me on a bus that gets to your town at 4:30 Friday afternoon. Dad will pick me up around 6:00 Sunday evening. Thanks for asking me!

Sincerely,
Tim

After the weekend with Pete, you must write a bread-and-butter (a thank you for hospitality) letter to Pete's mother. It might read something like this:

Dear Mrs. Morrison,

Thank you for inviting me for the weekend. I had a wonderful time. That was the biggest fish I *ever* caught. I hope Pete can catch a big one, too.

Sincerely,
Tim

(*51*)

Another kind of letter you have to write from time to time is a thank-you note for a gift that someone has sent you, usually from far away. Here's a thank-you letter:

Dear Grandma,

   Wow, that was a wonderful set of trucks that you sent me! I got a strong box and built a garage for them and I send them out on trips. Thanks a lot! I hope you'll be coming to see us soon.

Love,
Tim

Know-Your-Letter-Writing Quiz

Do you:

1. Tell your guest what time he is expected to arrive and leave?

2. Answer an invitation as soon as possible when you see RSVP written on it?

3. Write a bread-and-butter letter only if you have been a guest for a week or more?

(53)

4. Send a thank-you letter only to relatives?

5. Let your weekend guest know just what kind of clothes he should bring?

6. Extend an invitation only by letter?

7. Thank your friend for the invitation when you reply?

8. Send a bread-and-butter letter to your friend instead of to his mother?

Now turn the page upside down and see what your score is. If you have:

8 right: You know your letter writing!

5-7 right: Your mistakes indicate that you should read the chapter over once more.

1-4 right: You had better get out a pen and paper, and practice!

None right: Read the chapter over until you learn all the rules of letter writing.

ANSWERS

1. Y
2. Y
3. N
4. N
5. Y
6. N
7. Y
8. N

Etiquette on the Telephone

Of course, you know how to phone. You've been talking to your aunt and your best friend and other people for ages. But do you really know the *right* way to make a call, and how to answer the phone in your own house?

If your mother allows you to answer the phone, you should pick up the receiver and say hello pleasantly. You might also add, "David Jones speaking."

If the caller asks for your father say, "Just a moment, please." Lay the receiver down *very quietly* on the table, and go quickly to tell your father that he is wanted on the phone. (*Never*, as one child did, say all these polite things and then hang the receiver back on its hook!) If your father is not there, say "I'm sorry — my father isn't here just now. Would you like to leave a message for him?"

When you make a call to a friend, identify yourself immediately.

"This is David Jones; may I speak to Billy, please?"

The only other rule is: *Don't stay on the phone too long.* The other person may have something else to do. Or another member of your family may want to make a call.

Know-Your-Telephone-Manners Quiz

Do you:

1. Throw the receiver down on the table when the call is not for you?
2. Ask to take a message if someone is not at home?
3. Give your name when you call a friend?
4. Talk as long as you want to?
5. Answer the phone in a pleasant voice?
6. Have to say who you are when you answer the phone?

(58)

7. Hang up immediately if you find out that the call is not for you?

8. Remember that other people in your home want to use the phone, too?

Now turn the page upside down and see what your score is. If you have:

    8 right: You have excellent telephone manners.

5-7 right: Another look at this chapter should correct your mistakes.

1-4 right: You are not very sure of how to use a telephone.

None right: Read the chapter thoroughly until you know the rules of telephone use.

ANSWERS
1. N
2. Y
3. Y
4. N
5. Y
6. N
7. N
8. Y

Boy Etiquette Versus Girl Etiquette

Most of the rules of good manners apply to both boys and girls. But there are some differences. All children should stand up when an older person comes into the room, and remain standing until everyone is seated. But *boys* must stand whenever a girl comes into the room. And if there aren't enough seats to go around, he must always offer his to the girl.

A boy should open the door for a girl, and if they go out together he should help her on and off with her coat. Afterward, he should hold it when she puts it on again.

A boy holds a girl's chair when she is seating herself at the dinner table, pushing it in gently when she bends her knees. He never seats himself until all the girls are seated.

A boy always follows a girl down an aisle, or into a car,

(*60*)

or through most doors. He never shoves ahead. However, he does go first through a revolving door to push it for the girl, and he does get off a bus or train first, so that he may help her down the steps.

A boy carries packages for any woman or girl he is walking with. And he always walks on the curbside of the sidewalk.

Girls, in turn, wait for boys to perform these little courtesies. A girl who charges ahead and doesn't *let* a boy show his good manners is guilty of bad manners herself.

Know-Your-Boy-Girl-Etiquette Quiz

Do you:

1. Remain seated (if you are a boy) when a girl enters the room?

2. Seat yourself (if you are a boy) after all the girls are seated?

3. Wait (if you are a girl) for a boy to perform courtesies?

4. Stand up when an older person comes into the room?

5. Walk (if you are a boy) in front of a girl down the aisle?

6. Go first (if you are a boy) through a revolving door?

7. Expect (if you are a girl) that a boy will walk on the curbside of the sidewalk?

8. Carry packages (if you are a boy) for a girl or older woman?

Now turn the page upside down and see what your score is. If you have:

     8 right: You have manners!

  5-7 right: People will like to have you around more if you correct those mistakes.

  1-4 right: Perhaps you had better read the chapter over again.

None right: You need lots of practice to know your boy-girl etiquette.

ANSWERS

1. N
2. Y
3. Y
4. Y
5. N
6. Y
7. Y
8. Y

Your Ticket to Good Times

At the beginning of this book, we learned that "etiquette" comes from a French word that means "ticket." And knowing the rules of etiquette is your own personal ticket to good times. When you first read the rules, you may have thought that they were difficult and not much fun to learn. But read them over again. As soon as you know them, you will discover that an exciting thing has happened to you. Because when you know the rules of etiquette, you know how to act at a party, at a friend's house, or anywhere else. And when you know how to act properly, you can just relax and enjoy yourself anywhere.

So, read the rules of etiquette over and over until you know them. Remember, they are your own ticket to good times.

(66)

27480

Index

J395   HOKE   27480
            ETIQUETTE

HOKE

Date Due

NO 10 '70		
DE 5 '70		
JA 30 '71		
AG 4 '7		
DE 7 '73		
JE 6 '75		
MAY 3 1 1980		
JUN 1 9 1980		
SEP 1 0 1981		
AUG - 2 1989		
AUG 2 5 1989		

CANCELLED

SOUTHOLD FREE LIBRARY
SOUTHOLD, NEW YORK

97

PRINTED IN U.S.A.